SPORTS GAMES

BY DIANA MURRELL

Apex is distributed by North Star Editions:
sales@northstareditions.com | 888-417-0195

Produced for Apex by Red Line Editorial.

Photographs ©: Shutterstock Images, cover, 1, 4–5, 6–7, 8, 9, 16–17, 18, 19, 20–21, 22–23, 24–25, 26, 27; Paul Sakuma/AP Images, 10–11; Evan Amos/Wikimedia Commons, 12, 29; iStockphoto, 13; ArcadeImages/Alamy, 14–15

Library of Congress Control Number: 2022920690

ISBN
978-1-63738-577-7 (hardcover)
978-1-63738-631-6 (paperback)
978-1-63738-733-7 (ebook pdf)
978-1-63738-685-9 (hosted ebook)

Printed in the United States of America
Mankato, MN
082023

NOTE TO PARENTS AND EDUCATORS

Apex books are designed to build literacy skills in striving readers. Exciting, high-interest content attracts and holds readers' attention. The text is carefully leveled to allow students to achieve success quickly. Additional features, such as bolded glossary words for difficult terms, help build comprehension.

TABLE OF CONTENTS

CHAPTER 1

NHL FACE-OFF   4

CHAPTER 2

EARLY SPORTS GAMES   10

CHAPTER 3

GAMES TODAY   16

CHAPTER 4

ESPORTS   22

COMPREHENSION QUESTIONS • 28

GLOSSARY • 30

TO LEARN MORE • 31

ABOUT THE AUTHOR • 31

INDEX • 32

NHL FACE-OFF

A boy and his friend are playing *NHL 23*. The friends select players for their teams. They choose each player's position, too. Then the puck drops.

Many sports video games have multiplayer modes.

The boy's player speeds across the ice. His friend's player checks him and steals the puck. But the boy takes it back.

Each athlete in *NHL 23* has different skills. Some focus on shooting. Others play defense.

FAST FACT

Like many sports games, *NHL 23* lets players pick real pro athletes for their teams.

Many video games based on pro sports are updated every year. Each new version includes new players.

Next, the boy sends his player toward his friend's goal. His friend tries to stop him with her goalie. But he takes a slapshot and scores.

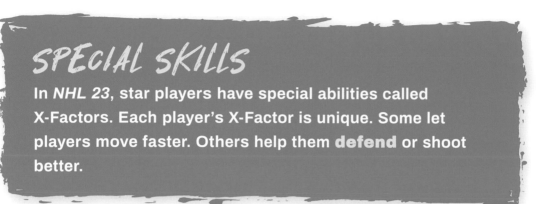

SPECIAL SKILLS

In *NHL 23*, star players have special abilities called X-Factors. Each player's X-Factor is unique. Some let players move faster. Others help them **defend** or shoot better.

Some X-Factors help players shoot the puck harder or aim to make tricky shots.

CHAPTER 2

EARLY SPORTS GAMES

The first sports video game was *Tennis for Two*. It was made in 1958. But *Pong* made the sports **genre** popular. This game came out in 1972. Many people played it.

Pong was based on table tennis. Players moved rectangles to bounce a ball back and forth.

Many early games featured team sports, such as basketball and soccer. People played some games at **arcades**. Others used **consoles** at home.

The Atari 2600 was a console made in the 1970s.

Arcade games were most popular in the late 1970s and early 1980s.

PLAYING TOGETHER

Early sports games were often multiplayer. For some games, players faced off. Other games had two players work together. Each player controlled part of the team.

In *Tony Hawk's Pro Skater* games, players do skateboard tricks.

In the 1980s and 1990s, companies added more sports. They also made new consoles and controllers. The new systems had better **graphics**.

FAST FACT

In 1991, Tecmo Super Bowl became the first game to use both real players and real teams.

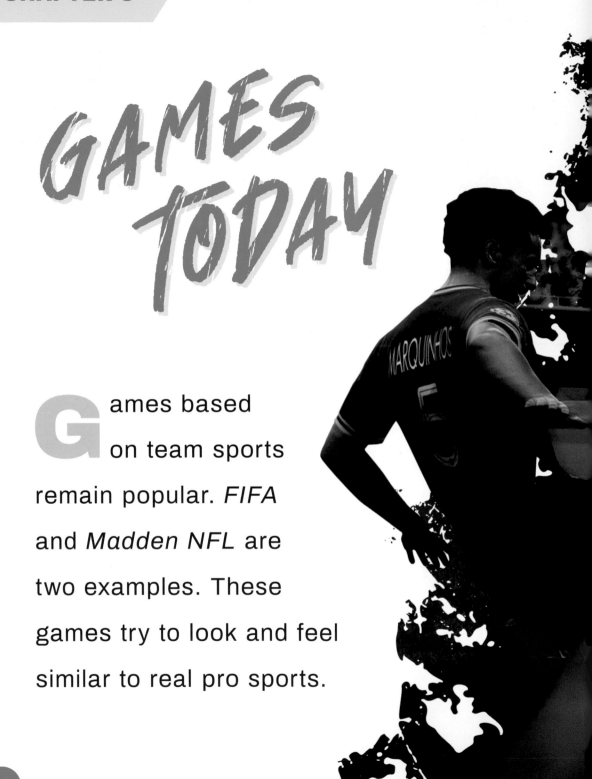

CHAPTER 3

GAMES TODAY

Games based on team sports remain popular. *FIFA* and *Madden NFL* are two examples. These games try to look and feel similar to real pro sports.

The *FIFA* series is the best-selling sports video game in the world.

In *Mario Kart*, players can race against one another or against a computer.

Racing games are popular, too. *Gran Turismo* lets players choose from more than 400 cars. In *Mario Kart*, players race go-karts.

FAST FACT

Wii Sports games use motion-sensing controllers. Players act out sports to play them.

A Nintendo Wii's controllers track how players move their hands.

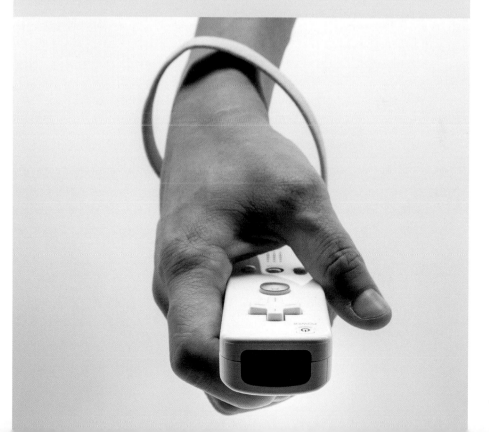

MANAGER 22™

In *F1 Manager*, players help a team build and race superfast cars.

Some sports games focus on management. Players are in charge of teams. They pick coaches and control the money. They also **recruit** and train team members.

F1 MANAGER

F1 Manager is a sports management game. It focuses on Formula 1 racing. Players train their teams' drivers. They also find **sponsors**. This helps their teams earn money.

CHAPTER 4

ESPORTS

Many sports gamers compete in **tournaments**. They try to beat other players and teams. Winners can earn millions of dollars in prizes.

Many tournaments draw large crowds. People gather to watch their favorite gamers.

Rush with a Run Play for 2

CHICAGO BEARS

+15%

41

B. Ce

The *Madden NFL* games are some of the best-selling video games in the United States.

Top games often have their own events. For example, the Madden Bowl takes place each year. At this tournament, gamers play *Madden NFL*. *FIFA* has tournaments, too.

FAST FACT

Some gamers get scholarships to play for colleges.

NBA 2K League is a popular esports league. Teams play weekly games and compete in tournaments.

Some gamers join esports leagues. Each gamer is part of a team. The teams compete in a series of games. Top gamers can get paid to play.

ROCKET LEAGUE

In *Rocket League*, players control rocket-powered cars. They play sports such as soccer and basketball. Players join matches online. They can also play in tournaments.

In *Rocket League*, players use cars to move the ball.

COMPREHENSION QUESTIONS

Write your answers on a separate piece of paper.

1. Write a few sentences explaining how sports games have changed over time.

2. Would you want to compete in a sports game tournament? Why or why not?

3. What was the first sports video game?

    A. *Tennis for Two*

    B. *Pong*

    C. *FIFA*

4. Why would gamers want better graphics?

    A. to help more people play games at the same time

    B. to help games look more like real-life sports

    C. to help games cost less money to make

5. What does **select** mean in this book?

The friends ***select*** *players for their teams. They choose each player's position, too.*

    A. lose something
    B. pick something
    C. forget something

6. What does **management** mean in this book?

Some sports games focus on ***management.*** *Players are in charge of teams.*

    A. having many fans
    B. being a top player
    C. being a leader

Answer key on page 32.

GLOSSARY

arcades
Places where people can play video games by putting coins into large machines.

consoles
Devices that people use to play video games at home.

defend
To try to stop the other team from scoring.

genre
A type or category of something.

graphics
The images players see during a game.

recruit
To get someone to join a team or group.

scholarships
Money given to students to help pay for education.

sponsors
People or companies who give money.

tournaments
Events where players try to win several games or rounds.

TO LEARN MORE

BOOKS

Abdo, Kenny. *NBA 2K*. Minneapolis: Abdo Publishing, 2022.

Bolte, Mari. *Madden NFL*. Chicago: Norwood House Press, 2022.

Rathburn, Betsy. *Console Gaming*. Minneapolis: Bellwether Media, 2021.

ONLINE RESOURCES

Visit **www.apexeditions.com** to find links and resources related to this title.

ABOUT THE AUTHOR

Diana Murrell is a writer and teacher. She lives in Canada with her family. Diana likes playing video games and exploring nature trails when she is not writing.

INDEX

A

arcades, 12

C

consoles, 12

F

F1 Manager, 21
FIFA, 16, 25

G

Gran Turismo, 18
graphics, 15

M

Madden NFL, 16, 25
management games, 21
Mario Kart, 18

N

NHL 23, 4, 6–9

P

Pong, 10

R

racing games, 18
Rocket League, 27

T

team sports, 12, 16
Tecmo Super Bowl, 15
Tennis for Two, 10
tournaments, 22, 25, 27

W

Wii Sports, 19

ANSWER KEY:
1. Answers will vary; 2. Answers will vary; 3. A; 4. B; 5. B; 6. C